A-Z Gui(

Third .

by Tim Moshansky

Published By First Wave Publishing
P.O. Box 71031
Vancouver, B.C. V6N 4J9

Printed in Canada
ISBN 0-9680702-1-3
9 780968 070215

This book is published without the help of any government subsidies or loans.

Forward

Welcome to the third edition of the A-Z Guide to Film Terms! When I started this I book I was fascinated by the exotic and mysterious language of film production. What began as a hobby turned into a full fledged obsession with film language, and has now become a lifelong pursuit. If I never become fluent in a foreign language, at least I know that I was somewhat conversant in "filmspeak," and it was certainly worth the effort. I hope you enjoy your foray into this world of terminology. Roll cameras, And...Action!

Tim Moshansky, Vancouver, B.C.

Acknowledgements

I would like to extend a special thank you to a number of people who have really helped make this book a success. Thanks to Jane Still for her neverending goodwill and for spreading the gospel of Timothy. Her support has been enormous. Thanks to my sister, Sheri Lee for proofreading the final text. Thanks also to Carmen Lane, the book's visual/text/layout/designer for her faithful support and patience with my procrastinations and last minute panic requests and demands, and to all of the bookstores, film schools, seminars, film commissions, guilds and unions who have integrated this book into their systems. Special thanks to Shane Harvey for his photography and to Kirk Johns for his illustrations.

This book is dedicated to my mother, Lavina, and to my sweetheart, Wendy.

Legend:

A-Z Guide to Film Terms

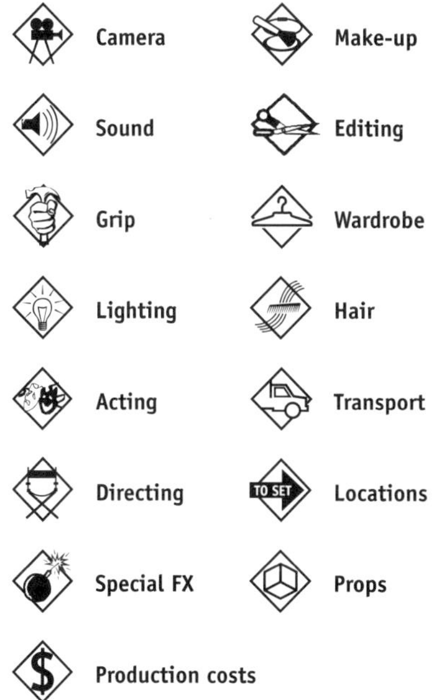

a

A/B Roll Using two video or film sources running at the same time to create editing effects such as dissolves and wipes.

Abby Singer Shot The second last shot of the day. This term supposedly comes from the 1st A.D. of the same name who would always say, "this is the last shot," when it really wasn't. See also *window shot*.

Above-the-line Production costs that involve the principal creative elements, such as the writer, director, producer and lead performers.

Academy Leader Eight-second countdown at the beginning of films standardised by the *Academy of Motion Picture Arts and Sciences*.

Ace One thousand watt (1k) light.

A.C.E. Association of Cinematic Editors.

A.C.F.C. Association of Canadian Film Craftspeople.

Action Command for the actors or technicians to begin their performance.

Action Prop Any property or device constructed to perform an action or movement or which has any animated function. The giant squid in *20,000 Leagues Under the Sea* is an action prop. Also called an *animated prop*.

A.C.T.R.A. Alliance of Canadian Cinema, Television and Radio Actors.

Actual Music See *source music*.

Actual Sound Sound that is heard by the characters in a film.

A.D. See *assistant director*.

A.D. Box Small room in the honeywagon trailer for use by the assistant directors, particularly the 3rd A.D., when on location to do paperwork, faxes to the office, etc.

Ad Lib When an actor or director improvises a scene or dialogue that is not in the script.

A.D.R. Automated Dialogue Replacement. The process of re-recording dialogue in a studio to replace or improve the sound quality. See also *looping*.

Aerial Shot A shot that is taken from above the ground with the help of a helicopter, blimp or plane.

Agent A person that represents an actor or performer in exchange for a percentage of the actor's wage or a flat fee. An agent typically negotiates the most money for their client because then they tend to make more.

A.K.S. Camera and sound term for a box that contains "all kinds of s**t," or "all kinds of stuff."

Alan Smithee When a director wants his or her name removed from the final credits of a production, usually because of a conflict with the producer or because the show is really awful, the name Alan Smithee is used in place of the director's real name.

Ambient Noise On a sound recording, noise often gets picked up other than the desired dialogue and sound effects, such as traffic, wind, etc. When recording on location, a mixer may record several seconds of ambient noise that reflects the character of the room or space, which is used in the editing process to create a more natural soundscape. Also called *room tone*.

Animatronics The area of special effects that deals with puppets of bears, dogs, aliens and humans that are animated with remote controlled servo motors.

Answer Print First print of a finished film which is printed with supposedly the correct timing for each shot.

Aperture The size of the hole that lets light into a lens, controlled by the iris.

Apollo A moving camera platform that is like a tulip crane mounted on the back of a truck. The truck can use electric power to move silently during a shot.

Apple Box Small rectangular box used by grips to elevate stands and other work gear. Sizes include full apple, half apple and quarter apple.

Aquarium The control booth or mixing room in a recording studio, named for its large window that looks into the recording room. Also called a *fishbowl*.

Arri Shortened trade name for Arriflex motion picture camera, taken from the first two letters of its inventors, Arnold and Richter.

Art Director Up until the 1970's, the Art Director was the person in charge of preparing and supervising all visual elements on a production. In today's film world, this position has been given the title *Production Designer.* An Art Director now works in most circumstances as an assistant to the PD.

A.S.C. American Society of Cinematographers. A.S.C. is "not a labour union or guild, but an educational, cultural and professional organisation." Membership is by invitation only.

Aspect Ratio The ratio of height to width in a video or film image.

Assembly The physical act of putting together a film or video.

Assistant Director (A.D.) Person(s) who acts as a liaison between the director and the rest of the crew to ensure that everything runs smoothly and on time. See *first assistant director, second assistant director, third assistant director and trainee assistant director.*

Assistant Locations Manager (A.L.M.) Person who oversees a location while shooting. The A.L.M. must possess good P.R. and problem solving skills, and usually has all the relevant information regarding a location such as where to find water, electricity, washrooms and telephones or where to park crew and unit vehicles. The A.L.M. also delegates responsibility to police officers and P.A.'s on set, organises company moves, babysits grumpy crew members and ensures that a location is properly cleaned upon completion of filming. When something goes wrong on a set, the A.L.M. is usually the first person to get dumped on. See also *location manager.*

Associate Producer In the increasingly complex world of filmmaking, sometimes it is hard to understand what each producer actually does. In most cases, an Associate Producer is someone who has been involved in one or more aspects of producing a movie, but is not given full producer credit.

Audition When a performer goes to try out for a role, whether it is for a voice-over or a principal role.

Auteur The "Auteur Theory" was created by French film critics of the 1960's. In a nutshell, it claims that a director who is an "auteur" (literally, "author") is incapable of making a bad film, that everything he or she has done, even if it is their high school project, is a masterpiece. Directors such as Hitchcock, Fellini and Truffaut are considered "auteurs."

A **Boom Operator** prepares to record sound with the boom pole at full extension.
Photo by Shane Harvey

b

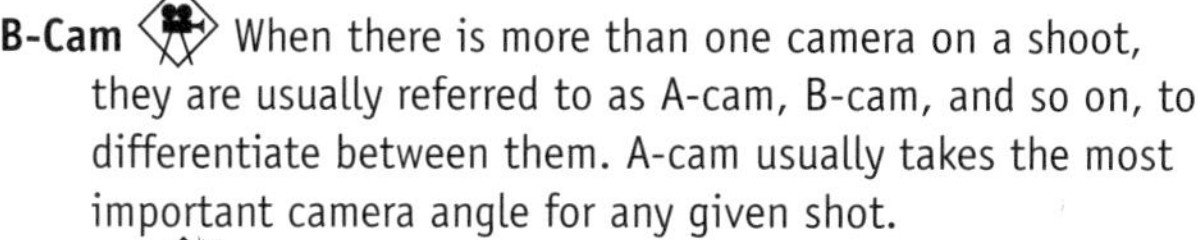

B-Cam When there is more than one camera on a shoot, they are usually referred to as A-cam, B-cam, and so on, to differentiate between them. A-cam usually takes the most important camera angle for any given shot.

B-Gum A sap from an Olibana tree that is used by special effects personnel to create steam and smoke effects by burning it. See *bee smoker*.

Babble Crowd background sound that is active and noisy. See also *murmur* and *walla*.

Baby 1) A 1000 watt Fresnel light. 2) A small stand or plate used by grips.

Baby Plate Small plate which can be screwed onto walls and ceilings to mount lights, bounce boards, etc.

Background Extras used in a scene to create a sense of realism.

Backlighting Lighting that comes from behind an actor, towards the camera.

Ballast A device that regulates the current from a power source to an HMI light.

Bamboolah A rectangular wooden frame with black cloth wrapped around it, used for controlling large unwanted areas of light.

Banana A move performed by the actors or the camera that is in a curved line. "Do a *banana* as you walk by the camera."

Barn Doors The metal doors that you see on the edges of lights, these can be adjusted to control the light from streaming out in all directions.

Barney A padded cover that fits over a camera to prevent camera noise from leaking through. Also called a *sound barney*.

Bazooka A long, pole-like device that is used for mounting light fixtures on catwalks.

Beachball See *sandbag*.

Beat A slight pause in speech or action.

Bee Smoker A device used for creating small puffs of white smoke, or for creating a hazy, smoke-filled atmosphere on set. These are the same units that bee keepers use to narcotise the bees in an apiary to prevent themselves from being stung.

Below-the-line Production costs that are not included in above the line costs, including crew, equipment, transportation, catering, and so forth.

Best Boy Next in command to a head of department, such as a Best Boy Grip, Lighting or Special Effects.

Betacam A high quality video camera developed and produced by Sony that is used primarily for television productions, ENG and commercials.

BFL Technical acronym for Big F#%*ing Light.

Big Four The "Big Four" US. television networks, as they are often referred to, are ABC, CBS, NBC and Fox.

Bigeye A 10,000 watt (10k) incandescent light.

Blimp See *barney*.

Blocking "Blocking the shot" is what the director, actors and heads of departments do to see the placement and movement of actors, vehicles etc., after which the actors take a break and the various departments set up lights, cameras, makeup and so on.

Blonde 2000 watt variable beam spotlight, named for its yellow colour.

Blue Screen An actor is filmed in front of a blue screen so that later a different background may be layered in behind him or her. This technique is also used for miniatures as well. (The "Star Wars" space battle scenes were accomplished using blue screen technology.) See also *composite*.

Body Mic See *wire*.

Bogie Someone or something (usually a pedestrian or vehicle) that gets in the way of the shot. "Get that *bogie* out of there now!"

Bolex Swiss-made 16mm film camera, known for its ease of operation and dependability.

Boned Technical term used when something is potentially screwing up and/or delaying some aspect of production. "We're gonna be *boned* if we don't get this shot before sunset."

Boom An extendible pole that holds a microphone to record dialogue and sound effects on a set.

Boom Op Person who operates the microphone boom, a long, extendible rod with a microphone attached to the end.

Boom Shot A shot where the camera rises or lowers vertically on a platform. See also *crane shot*.

Boot Padded cylindrical sleeve that fits over the viewfinder arm on noisy cameras to prevent sound leakage.

Bosun's Chair A chair attached to a series of pulleys and ropes that can be hung with a camera operator inside to get shots over a river or waterfall, or anywhere a jib arm or dolly track can't go.

Bounce Board A white piece of cardboard or styrofoam used to "bounce" light onto a subject from a direct source, such as the sun or a powered light.

Bounce Light Like a lot of motion picture lighting, this is light that is bounced off of a reflective surface onto a subject.

Breakaway Anything that is designed to break apart easily without causing harm to the actors. You often see breakaway chairs and tables in barroom fights in movies.

Breakaway Glass Special glass that is used for stunts and special effects, such as when you see an actor or stuntman crash through a plate glass window. It is essentially special tempered glass that breaks in small pieces rather than dangerous shards. See also *sugar glass.*

Breakdown A scene by scene analysis of a film or video used to determine production requirements and scheduling.

Break the bubble A term used to describe the tilting of a camera off of the horizontal axis. See also *dutch angle.*

Briefcase Dolly A small, self contained dolly that can be used as a camera or hauling dolly, and packs right up into its own case!

Brute 1) A large flag used for cutting off light. 2) A carbon arc light, broken down into a baby brute and a lite weight brute.

Buck A car or other vehicle that has its top removed for doing interior shots.

Buck and a Half Camera term for 150mm lens.

Buffalo Box Camera housing used to protect a camera when being hand held in rough situations, such as on rollerblades. Also called a *crash box*.

Burned Location TO SET Any location (house, restaurant, park or whatever) that will not allow filming due to previous problems with film crews. Sometimes the result of just too much shooting being done there, a location can also be burned by loud and obnoxious crew members, unfulfilled cash promises, moving trucks in or out after curfew or a multitude of other reasons.

Burn-in Titles or subtitles that are laid on top of an existing film or video image. Once done, these titles cannot be removed, hence the name.

Butt Plug Small metal cylindrical peg that is used to mount small lights.

Butterfly Adjustable board of various sizes attached to two stands so it can be angled to reflect or bounce light.

Buyer A person responsible for buying props or set decorations for the art department of a production company.

Buyout $ The amount of money paid to an actor in addition to his or her rate that "buys out" the residual pay that would normally come with repeated showings of a tv commercial or tv show.

C-Stand From "Century-stand," this is one of the most useful and used pieces of grip/lighting equipment there is. This "workhorse of the movie industry" has three staggered legs which can be folded under each other in a line for easy storage.

Cable Puller A person in the sound department who is in charge of microphone cables (that sometimes need to be pulled out of the way on moving shots) and wiring of actors. Also called a *sound assistant* or *assistant sound mixer.*

Call Back After a performer goes for an audition, a call back is a sign that he or she were interesting enough to be short-listed, and are requested to come for a subsequent audition. Sometimes an actor may be called back several times before securing a role.

Call Sheet Sheet given out at the end of each day outlining the crew call time for each crew member, and also contains location maps and other production requirements for the next day of shooting.

Call Time The time at which the cast and crew must show up for work on the set. Some crew members may have different call times than others. See also *crew call.*

Cameo A brief appearance or performance (usually by a celebrity) in a film or tv program. Alfred Hitchcock can be seen in a cameo appearance in almost every single one of his films.

Camera Truck The truck that houses all of the exposed and unexposed film in coolers, as well as various camera accessories. Usually parked as close to the set as possible.

Cans Slang term for headphones worn by boom operators and sound mixers.

Captain See *transport captain*.

Carps Slang for carpenters, those employed in building the sets.

Cast People portraying the characters in a movie or television program.

Casting The process of finding actors to fill the various roles in a film, usually headed by a casting director.

Casting Couch A reference to the piece of furniture that an aspiring actress or actor has sex on with a director or casting agent in order to secure a role in a film.

Cattle Call A general call for actors or extras.

Catwalk Platforms or decks that are mounted up near the ceiling in many studios. See also *greens*.

Cel A single sheet of celluloid that is used in animation.

Charlie Bar A long, slender flag used by grips to shade light off a specific area.

Cheat To purposely move an object or actor in or out of the way in coverage shots that may not be exact in continuity, but done in a way so no-one will notice in the final edited version of a film. (e.g. "*Cheat* that table this way a bit so we can see his body more.")

Check the Gate The 1st A.D. asks for the camera assistant to "check the gate" when the director has gotten the shot he needs and is ready to move on to the next shot, or wrap for the day. This is done to ensure that the camera gate is clear of small hairs, film shards and other debris.

Cheese Plate A grip term for a metal plate with holes in it that can be used to mount lights, etc. onto almost any surface.

Chicken Coop An overhead, box-like multiple light set, usually used for top lighting of sets.

Chimera A small, portable light in a nylon housing. This "soft" light is often used to follow an actor during a moving shot.

Cinema Verité A genre of cinema that attempts to be as realistic as possible.

Circus TO SET The area where the majority of trucks, trailers, tents and catering trucks are set up while filming on location.

The Circus *Illustration by Kirk Johns*

Clapper Small black and white board with spaces for the title of the production, the scene number, the take number, the director and cameraman's name, and the name of the production company producing the film. The top of the board has a stick that is clapped together to create a sound and picture reference mark used to synchronise the two later in post production. See also *slate*.

Claw A device within the camera that pulls the film through by the perforations on the side of the film.

Clean Shot When two actors are facing each other during dialogue scenes, the camera will have a clean angle on each from the angle of the facing actor. A shot is "clean" when the actor facing camera is alone in the frame, and the other actor is off camera. A shot is "dirty" when it contains part of the actor with his back to the camera, also called an "over the shoulder" shot.

Closed Set For filming a scene that requires actor nudity or an intense emotional commitment, the director will call for a "closed set," in which only the absolutely essential crew members (such as the camera and boom operator) may be present.

Clunker Box A device used for sequentially firing lights, squibs or explosions. The predecessor of the clunker box is the nail board, which some special effects people still prefer.

Cobweb Juice Liquid, glue-like solution used by special effects people to create cobwebs.

Cobweb Spinner A drill-like device with fan blades attached to it that is used for creating cobwebs.

Coffin Light A set of lights arranged with a black curtain around them for soft lighting of a scene.

Coke and a Smoke When the director wants a private blocking or rehearsal with the actors, the crew is asked to go for a "coke and a smoke," i.e. leave the set and take a break.

Cold Reading Reading a script or line without seeing it or previously rehearsing it.

Colour Bars A standard set of colours arranged in bars on a t.v. screen used to achieve an accurate colour setting. You sometimes see these on t.v. when you wake up on the couch at 4 a.m.

Colour Temperature A method of determining the colour of a light by its temperature. This temperature is measured in the Kelvin scale, which is the same as the metric Celsius scale, but with a different starting point. (0° K=–273° Centigrade).

Commentative Sound Sound heard only by the audience, not by the characters in a film. This includes background music and narration.

Company Move TO SET When shooting on location, sometimes it is necessary to move the entire crew and all of the trucks to a new location. This may sound easy but more closely approximates organised confusion. Not to be confused with a mini move.

Composite Two or more images that have been layered

together to form a single image. This technique is often used for special effects.

Com-Tek Small device used to receive an audio signal so the director and other key personnel can monitor the dialogue and sound as they are being recorded.

Condor Large, movable crane-like device with a bucket on an extending arm to elevate cameras, lights and/or operators. Not to be confused with the Robert Redford movie "Three Days of the Condor."

Continuity The flow of narrative within a film. If continuity is not right, audiences are left wondering what happened from one edit to the next.

Contrapuntal Music Background music that is not synchronised to the image on the screen, but runs its own course, as if it were telling its own version of the story. See *Mickey Mousing*.

Cookie Cutter See *cuculoris*.

Co-Producer Someone who shares the producer credit for a movie or tv program with someone else.

Co-Production A production that is jointly produced by two enities, whether they are corporations, countries or individuals.

Copy Walkie-talkie talk for: "I understood your message," or, "Got it." "Do you copy that?"

Costume Designer Person who, in consultation with the director and production designer, designs, creates or acquires all wardrobe and costumes needed for a production. They also ensure that extra sets of clothing in the right sizes are available for stunt and photo doubles and stand-ins.

Costumer You will often find this person in the wardrobe trailer organising and issuing costumes to actors and extras. Other duties include washing and drying and ironing of costumes.

Costume Supervisor Person who is in charge of all wardrobe requirements on a set. They check wardrobe continuity before shooting, do "final touches," and keep the actors warm and dry between takes. They also assist in the final decision as to what the extras will wear while on set.

Coverage During a shoot, getting "coverage" refers to the amount of angles and viewpoints captured on film that can be used in the editing process to give a scene pace, variety and movement.

Cover Set TO SET A pre-dressed studio or location set that sits waiting and is used to "cover" for a production in case of bad weather or logistical problems.

Cowboy Shot A medium wide shot of an actor from head to about halfway between his or her waist and knees. This term comes from the western movies, where a shot would frame the cowboy from the top of his head to just below his gun and holster.

Crab Dolly Four-wheeled camera dolly that can move in any direction (including sideways, like a crab).

Craft Service 1) The area (usually a table) where all kinds of food and drink are served on a continual basis all day long for everyone in the cast and crew. You can generally find crew members who aren't currently busy grazing in this area. 2) The person on the set who has industrial first aid training for any accidents or injuries that may occur, and who prepares and serves foods and snacks to the crew throughout the working day. Also may be shown on the call sheet as FACS, CSFA, or Craft Service/First Aid.

Crane Shot A shot which is achieved by raising the camera and operator(s) with a crane or similar device.

Crew Call That point in time when the majority of the crew is on the set and working–"on the clock," as it were.

Crystal Sync True, reliable 24 frames per second camera speed.

CTB Colour Temperature Blue. A lighting term that refers to the colour of gel used in front of lights.

CTO Colour Temperature Orange. Another lighting term referring to the colour of gel sheet put in front of a light. CTOs and CTBs come in full, half, quarter and one eighth, which describes their relative colour temperature.

C.U. Close-up.

C.S.C. Canadian Society of Cinematographers.

Cuculoris Patterned flag that is used to create shadow patterns on backgrounds and subjects. Lighting directors frequently use them to simulate sunlight filtering through

trees. Also called a *cookie cutter*, or *cukaloris*.

Cue A signal for an actor, stuntman or extra to begin movement or speech.

Cue Card Large board with writing on it, usually lines or prompts for the actors.

Cue Sheet During the editing process, a cue sheet is used to keep track of the sequence of edits, the times, various tracks of sound and dialogue and so forth.

Cut 1) What the director yells when he wants the cameras and sound to stop rolling. 2) An edit in a film or video.

Cutaway A shot or edit that literally cuts away from the primary action, used to relieve tension or boredom during a scene.

Cutter 1) An editor, or someone who "cuts" and splices the film. 2) A rectangular device used for cutting off light on a set. See also *flag*.

Cutting room floor Where you and your ego end up if an editor cuts you out of a film.

Cyclorama (Cyc) A large, curved backdrop used to represent sky in a studio.

Cyc-strip A long strip of lights used for even illumination of a cyclorama.

Dailies Unedited, raw footage, usually shown in a small screening room to the producers, directors, and other key personnel to see if what they filmed the previous day is acceptable.

Dance Floor Smooth, pristine sheets of plywood that are screwed onto less expensive plywood for the camera dolly to move on.

Dash Card Card used to identify crew members' cars while filming on location.

D.A.W. Digital Audio Workstation. A state of the art editing system that can edit digital sound and pictures into finished, complete productions using just a computer.

Day for Night Shooting a scene during the day which actually appears in the movie as a night scene. This may be done in a variety of ways, including using different film stock, filters or developing procedures, or if shooting indoors, by blanketing out all windows and doors and lighting accordingly. Often appears as D/N on call sheets.

Day out of Days A document prepared by the A.D. department that lists each day in a production and a brief description of scenes, including actors and locations required.

Day Mo Crew member working on the set on a temporary, daily basis. A slightly condescending term.

Deal Memo The contract you sign with a production company prior to beginning work that outlines how much you will be paid, what screen credit you will receive and other details.

Deep Focus A process developed in the 1940's with faster film and more powerful lighting, making it possible to keep a greater depth of a scene in focus, even in interiors.

Deferral A contract method (often used by low budget producers) used to defer wages to cast and crew and equipment payments until a film has been released and makes a profit.

Depth of Field The amount of focus of near and distant objects in a camera lens.

Descender A device developed by British paratroopers to control the rate of descent, which is now used by special effects people.

Desert Dolly Sometimes called by its trade name, the Mojave Desert Dolly has big balloon tires that can travel over sandy beaches, deserts and other loose earth. Primarily used for lighting and grip equipment more than as a camera dolly.

Desmond A T-stop of 2.2, i.e.. two two, named for the South African Nobel Prize winner Desmond Tutu. This term originated in South Africa but has since travelled to North America and is widely used today.

D.G.A. Director's Guild of America.

D.G.C. Director's Guild of Canada.

Diffusion A reduction in the intensity of a light, or the device that does this (e.g. opal, litegrid, 216, frost).

Direct Cut A cut that is used for geographical or temporal (time) leaps in a film. It is also called an *impact cut*.

Director The head honcho. The big cheese. The auteur. The director, as we all know, is the person ultimately responsible for the look, sound and emotional impact of a film. He or she is the person who assembles a cast and crew often totaling over a hundred people to assist them in creating their vision of the film. A director directs the action of the actors, consults with the wardrobe, effects, lighting, grip, art, sound and locations department heads and with the help of the director of photography places the camera(s) in various positions to shoot scenes that will eventually be edited into a complete motion picture.

Dissolve Two shots that overlap each other in a final print are called a dissolve. The term can also be used as a verb, as in, "the shot of the car *dissolves* into the close-up of her face."

Distribution Once a film or tv show has been completed, it becomes necessary to distribute the product to networks and theatres for broadcast. In many cases, a show will already have a distribution deal in place before they start production.

Ditty Bag Small bag used by film crews to store little tools and other items. This term arose from sailors who carried a ditty bag of necessary items while at sea.

Diving Board Small wooden platform that attaches to the front or side of a dolly for a camera operator to stand on, hence the term. It also extends ahead of the dolly and is not used as commonly as the regular "side board".

Dolly Platform on wheels that has a mount for a camera, and can be pushed or pulled to create a smooth movement. Dollies are often put on tracks, and the camera and operator(s) ride with it. A crab dolly is a complex unit that can do tricky steering maneuvers and can rise up and down via hydraulics.

Dolly Grip Grip crew member specialising in camera movements via dollies of various kinds.

Dolly Track A tubular track that is used to guide a camera dolly for smooth "tracking" shots.

Donut Small, round pad with a hole in it that fits over the eyepiece of a viewfinder, or the larger round pad that fits between the matte box and lens of a camera to prevent light from getting in.

D.O.P. Director of Photography. A D.O.P. works closely with the lighting and camera departments to create the images that will eventually appear onscreen. Also called a *DP*.

Doorway Dolly A small, wagon like dolly that is steered by a pull handle. Used for cameras and operators.

Dot Miniature scrim placed in front of a light to control small specific areas.

Double 1) A member of the cast who "doubles," or impersonates the real actor. See also photo double and stunt double. 2) Grip term for a net diffusion, with 2 pieces overlapped. 3) Lamp Op term for a wire scrim.

Double Dip To work on two shows (and therefore collect two paycheques) at the same time.

Dress To decorate and arrange items such as furniture, drapes and artwork on a set.

Drive-by A shot where a camera shoots a stationary subject from a moving vehicle.

Dry run A rehearsal of a scene without shooting any film.

Dubbing 1) Replacing sound with a more complete, or better soundtrack mix. 2) The replacement of foreign dialogue in film with English, or vice-versa.

Duece A two-thousand watt (2k) light.

Dulling Spray A spray used on shiny surfaces such as windows and mirrors to prevent unwanted reflections.

Duster Slang term for a western/cowboy film.

Dust Gun A gun used by special effects people to create clouds of dust on a set.

Dutch Angle An exaggerated camera angle tilted to the rightor left of the horizontal line, popularised by early Dutch film-makers. Also called an *oblique angle*.

Dutch Head Tripod head that can pan, tilt and rock at angles other than 90 degrees. Also called a *rock and roll head*, this unit is very popular for rock videos.

Duvetyne Trade name for fire retardant black cloth that is used by grips on flags and windows to block out light.

D.V.E. Digital video effects.

E.C.U. Extreme close-up.

Edge of Frame The extent to which the camera lens sees in every direction.

Editing The assembling of images and sound into a completed production. One of the least understood aspects of production, editing is an extremely important part of the filmmaking process. It is here that the program is shaped and molded into its final form.

Editor A person who is involved in any part of the assembling of raw images and sound into a final product. There are a myriad of different types of editors, including dialog, special effects and music editors for sound and dozens of people involved with picture editing.

E.F.P. Electronic field production. E.F.P. is known for having somewhat better production values than E.N.G.

Eighty Six (86) To take something away. E.g. "We'll have to *86* the catering truck before the next setup." This term comes from bylaw 86 in Los Angeles which stipulates that film crews had to be out of residential neighbourhoods by a certain time.

Electronic Press Kit (E.P.K.) A press kit that is in the form of a video. A small crew, usually consisting of an interviewer, cameraman and sound person, shoot promotional footage and "behind the scenes" segments on movie sets for television shows (like "E.T.") or "the making of" programs.

Elevator Shot A shot that involves moving the camera on a platform vertically up or down, but not horizontally.

E.N.G. Electronic news gathering. Phrase used to describe the film news team style of production. E.N.G. footage is often shot with a Digital Betacam.

Episodic A series of televised programs that is filmed one episode after another for a "season" at a time.

Establishing Shot Usually the first shot in a scene, this shot gives the audience a reference point as to where a scene is taking place, like a high shot of the outside of a building.

Executive Producer The credit given to someone who either contributes or raises the majority of finances for a production or is responsible for creative input such as writing the screenplay or creating a series idea.

EXT. Exterior A shot that takes place outdoors.

Extra A person who is cast in a production, but who has no spoken lines. Extras are sometimes referred to as background, or background extras.

Extras Holding The place where extras are held until they are required for a scene.

Eyelight A small light which is used to create highlights in an actor's eyes.

Eyeline Where an actor is looking during a take. It is important to keep his or her eyeline clear during filming to avoid possible disruption of concentration.

Eyemo Small 35mm camera body that is used primarily for running at very high speeds for slow-motion photography.

F-stop Represents the light transmitting capabilities of a lens, a number of measurement obtained by dividing the focal length of a lens by its aperture.

Fade-In/Out A fade from a black or white background into a video or film image or vice-versa.

F.D.R. Another term for new deal, to signify that a shot has been completed and the crew is moving on to something else. This term arose from the fact that Franklin D. Roosevelt supposedly would always call for a new deal while he was president.

Feature A movie length film that is shown in movie houses or released on video. A feature is usually shot on 35mm film and is around 90 minutes long.

Fernie Another term for furniture pad, an all purpose pad used by grips to protect furniture, camera equipment or actors, and by the sound dept. to deaden unwanted noise.

Fill Light An extra light used to add, or fill areas of a set not lit by a key light.

Filmic Time The measurement of time as it occurs to the characters in a film that may only take a fraction of actual time to watch.

Film Noir Film genre which deals with dark subject matter, often characterised by moody lighting and music.

Final Touches The 1st A.D. calls for final touches just before the camera will roll, giving the set dec, wardrobe, hair, make-up and prop departments a last chance to tweak their subjects.

Finger Miniature scrim placed in front of a light to control small specific areas.

Fire Watch When a crew breaks for lunch, a P.A. is assigned to watch the set and all of the equipment to ensure nothing is stolen or damaged. This term harks back to the old studio days when there was a danger of fire starting out and burning everything down.

First Assistant Director (1st A.D.) The person responsible for ensuring that all of the departments are organised, co-ordinated and logistically ready for shooting scenes on a movie set. In pre-production they prepare a script breakdown and shooting schedule in consultation with the department heads. On set they assist the director by arranging all of the details so they can concentrate on the actors and the scene itself. They can often be identified by the headsets they wear to communicate with the crew, or as the person who calls out, "roll sound," "roll cameras," "cut," "reset," or "that's a wrap folks."

First Positions Return to your original positions after a cut. This term applies to actors, animals, extras and vehicles.

First Team The main actors. The 1st A.D. calls for the first team when everything is set and ready to roll.

Fishbowl See *aquarium*.

Fishpole Slang name for a boom, or microphone pole.

F.I.Z. Camera term for focus, iris, zoom.

Flag Square Black flag in a metal frame used to totally block out sections of light.

Flame Bar Long bar with handle that is used by special effects crews to simulate fire and flames in a controlled manner.

Flare An unwanted bright reflection that shows up on film.

Flashback A segment of a film which refers back to an earlier part of the narrative.

Flat A lightweight, movable 4′ x 8′ wooden structure that is used as part of a wall or backdrop in a studio or set.

Flatbed Another term for a Steenbeck editing table.

Flub To accidentally miss or screw up a line of dialogue.

Fluid Head A tripod head that uses a fluid to aid in smooth camera movements.

Fly To hang lights or rigging from the ceiling of a studio.

Flying in Phrase used by crew members to let someone know that they are on their way in to a set immediately.

Flying Moon A large lighting unit that houses four 25k HMIs and is raised above a set 100 feet or so to simulate artificial moonlight.

Focal Length The distance from the optical centre of the lens to the filmplane when the lens is focused at infinity.

Focus Puller Camera assistant who adjusts the focus of the lens while filming, often needed because the camera operator simply can't do everything at once. Also known as *1st camera assistant.*

Fog Filter A filter placed over the camera lens to simulate fog on film.

Foley Named after its creator, Jack Foley, this is the art of creating sound effects in a recording studio, whether walking on various surfaces to create footstep sounds, or clanging glasses in a bar scene in time to the action on the screen.

Foley Artist Person who creates Foley sounds for a film.

Foley Stage A room in a recording studio used for recording Foley sounds. It usually has a series of square panels on the floor which, when removed, reveal different textured surfaces such as concrete, sand, gravel and hard wood for a foley artist to match footstep sounds.

Follow-shot Any shot which follows an actor or vehicle, whether with panning, dollying, or any combination of movement.

Footage The amount of film used during a shoot is measured by the foot. "Hey, we got some great footage of that explosion yesterday!"

Foot Candle Measurement of the intensity of a light source.

Forced Call When a production manager needs to bring in a cast and crew without giving them a specific amount of time between wrap and their call time the next morning or over a weekend. To compensate for this, the crew and cast being "forced" are paid a premium rate for the entire day.

Foreground Anything that is in the front of a camera's field of vision and not blocked by anything else.

fps Frames per second.

Frame 1) The perimeter of vision recorded by a camera. 2) A single rectangular image on celluloid.

Freeze Frame An image that has been stopped during a moving picture, allowing viewers to view a "frozen" image. The freeze frame is often used behind the titles or credits of a film or t.v. show.

French Flag A small, opaque shade for shielding the camera lens.

French Hours A shooting day that allows for a one-hour sit down breakfast followed by nine hours of shooting without a break, at which point wrap is called. Food is served to the crew at various points during the day, and they grab a quick bite as they are working. This arrangement was developed and popularised in Europe, but is also used in North America to get a production back on schedule after an extremely long day, or for lighting reasons. Also called *Pacific Northwest Hours*.

Fresnel 1) A type of convex lens used for focusing lights. 2) A light equipped with a Fresnel lens. (pronounced fre-nell.)

Frost An opaque sheet of plastic in a frame used to diffuse a light source.

Fuller's Earth A non-toxic, clay-based earth used on movie sets as a double for real dirt.

Futz To alter or add sound to a dialogue track to make it sound like the voice is coming over the radio or a telephone.

F/X See *special effects*.

g

Gaffer The person in charge of all electrical and lighting requirements on set. This name comes from the early days of theatre in Britain, when all of the lighting was provided by candles. The lighting person would use a long stick called a gaff to light all of the candles, and was therefore called a "gaffer." His son, whom he would teach the trade, was called the "best boy."

Gag A joke, effect or contraption that is employed during a shot.

Gag Reel An edited portion of out-takes from a production, usually shown to the crew at wrap parties or at the end of a shooting schedule.

Gak General film term for equipment, props, etc. "Keep an eye on that gak so no-one touches it."

Gak Truck See *slush truck*.

Gaffer Tape Strong, silver-coloured tape used by grips and other departments.

Gels Coloured gelatin sheets that are placed in front of lights to change colour or colour intensity.

Genny Generator. A very important piece of film equipment– without it not much could be done on a modern film set (i.e. power for lights, fans, hair dryers, etc.).

Genny Operator Person in charge of running and maintaining the generator.

Gimbal Platform used to simulate movement in any type of vehicle, whether it is a car, plane, boat or spaceship.

Gimmick Light A small bulb used for hiding in confined spaces. Also called a *peanut bulb*.

Giraffe Boom A flexible microphone boom on a tripod used in studio situations as opposed to a fishpole.

Glow Light A very weak light source used to make an actor's face glow.

Gobo 1) Any shield or device that keeps light from directly striking the camera lens. 2) A free-standing structure used to disperse sound in any given environment.

Gobo Arm A thin, cylindrical extension arm to raise flags, etc. Usually mounted on a C-stand with a knuckle.

Gobo Ball A small rubbery ball that fits on the end of a gobo arm to prevent injuries to the cast and crew.

Go to "2" When communicating with walkie talkies, channel "1" is reserved for the entire crew to give short requests and commands to each other. When a longer conversation is required or when the topic does not concern everybody, you may hear someone say, "go to 2," which means change your radio to channel two.

Greek To change a sign so it reads differently or cannot be read at all. "If we can't get permission to use their sign we'll greek it before we go."

Green Light When a project has been given the go ahead and has the necessary funding in place to begin production. "We've received the *green light* on the feature we've been working on, and we begin production next month."

Green Room Traditionally the room where the talent waits before a performance or television appearance.

Green Screen See *blue screen*.

Greens 1) The department responsible for foliage, shrubs and other handling of "green" material that will be a part of a shot. 2) Another word for the catwalks or decks high in the rafters of Hollywood studios, so named because they were painted green.

Griff Large, square material mounted on a frame to reflect or absorb light. Also known by its trade name, Griffolyn.

Grip Crew member whose tasks include setting up and tearing down of various stands, dolly tracks, flats, flags, etc. There are several types of grips, including key grip, dolly grip, best boy grip, rigging grip, etc.

Gripology Any knowledge or information pertaining to the craft of gripping.

Griposaurus Another name for the large grip cart on wheels that contains flags, clamps, tape and many other gripology items that is kept as close to set as possible.

Groucho A cameraman asks an actor to do a "groucho" when he wants them to crouch as they walk. Inspired, of course, by the late, great Groucho Marx.

Guerrilla Filmmaking Producing a film or video without proper permits, insurance or location permission. This type of production is usually done with small crews with little or no budget who set up their cameras anywhere and start rolling.

Guide Track (G.T.) Sound track that is recorded on a set that will be used as a guide only in the editing or A.D.R. process, because of unavoidable noise such as rain, wind or mechanical sounds.

Guide Wire A small wire that is attached to an actor to guide an arrow or knife into their body to give the impression of the weapon actually hitting them.

Gyro Arm A camera device that uses a gyroscope to achieve a fluid, floating movement.

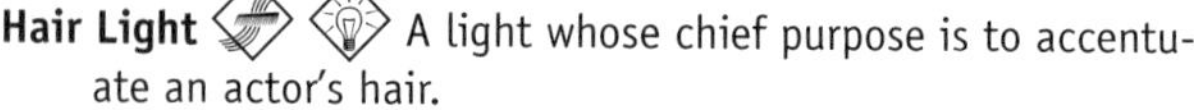

Hair Light A light whose chief purpose is to accentuate an actor's hair.

Hand Crank A camera that runs on a spring wound system rather than electric power, such as a 16mm Bolex.

Hand held A shot where the camera is carried on an operator's shoulder rather than mounted on a tripod or dolly.

HDTV High Definition Television, sometimes called "High Def".

Headroom The space between an actor's head and the top of the frame.

Hefty Herman A device that has a small platform that can be raised straight up about 20 feet with a light or a camera operator on it.

Hero A prop, car or element that is the featured item during shooting. For example, while shooting a toy commercial, many toys may be used during the day, but only one is the hero toy, or the one that is polished and perfect for filming purposes.

Hero Room A room that will actually be used while filming in a hotel, house or other building.

Hiatus A break or temporary hold on a production. Many t.v. series go on *hiatus* for the Christmas holidays.

Hi Hat A small camera mount screwed to a piece of wood for doing shots that are extremely low to the ground or other surface.

HMI Hydrargyum Medium Arc-Length Iodide, Halogen Metal Iodide, or Hydrogen Mercury Incandescent, depending on who you talk to. An HMI is a blue colour temperature light used to artificially reproduce sunlight on film.

H.O.D. Head of Department.

Hold the Roll Stop the action temporarily (i.e., until a car goes by or a cloud passes across the sun.)

Honeywagon The film unit trailer that contains the washrooms, A.D. box and other portable rooms.

Horse Opera An old term for a western movie.

Hot TO SET A gun or explosion that is loaded and will be used in an upcoming scene. Special effects or prop people won't go "hot" on a gun or squib until the very last minute on a film production.

Hot Head Could be a name for an angry crew member, but actually refers to a remote control camera mount that is attached to the end of a crane, ceiling or other place where a cameraman can't go.

Hot Set A set that needs to stay exactly the way it is for the continuity of shooting, either after lunch or on a later date. In other words, don't touch anything.

Hydroflex A completely waterproof camera housing unit.

IATSE International Alliance of Theatrical and Stage Employees.

IBEW International Brotherhood of Electrical Workers.

Incident Light Meter An exposure meter which measures the incident light falling on a subject from all angles. Developed in the 1940's by Don Norwood, this unit remains a common tool for cinematographers.

Inker Animation artist who draws details and outlines with acetate ink that is applied to the cels.

Inky Dink Small, focusable studio lamp with a 250 watt bulb and a Fresnel lens.

In the Can A finished, completed project. "Yeah, that one's in the can now. I'm just waiting for funding on my next project."

Insert Car Vehicle used to tow the action car for moving shots. Camera and lights are usually mounted on the insert car. See also *tow shot*.

Insert Shot Brief shot of an object, such as a clock, that is "inserted" briefly into an edited segment of a film or video.

INT. Interior. A shot is always designated as INT. or EXT. in a script to help determine production requirements and costs.

j

Jack Lord Camera term for a 50mm lens. (Five-0, you get it?) Book 'em, Danno.

Jib Arm A mechanical arm that has a camera at one end and a box of weights at the other, used to do sweeping shots—high or low, forward or backward. You often see jib arm shots in rock videos or in big budget t.v. specials like the Oscars. Often the camera has a remote control hot head or power pod attached to it to do pans and tilts.

Jog To move a video or film image in short spurts during the editing or viewing process.

Juice Electricity.

Juicer A person in the electrical or lighting department.

Jump Cut A cut that appears to jump, or mismatch between shots in a scene. An example of this is a shot of a man smoking a cigarette that jumps to a shot of him without the cigarette. Unless done for a specific reason, a jump cut is considered a glaring technical imperfection, especially to sophisticated viewers that have grown up on television and film.

Junior 1) A focusable studio lamp with a Fresnel lens and 2000 watt bulb, this is one of the most common studio lighting units. 2) A small C-stand.

k

k Kilowatt. Used to denote the power output of a light source. (e.g., 12k, 4k, or 2k)

Keeper A shot or take that will most likely be used in a film. If a shot is called a "keeper" by a director, it usually means that no additional takes will be required.

Kelvin A measurement of colour temperature.

Key Grip Person in charge of the grip department responsible for overseeing dolly track placement, lighting diffusion and other grip tasks.

Key Light Main light used to illuminate a set.

Kicker 1) A light source positioned behind and to the side of a subject, usually on the side opposite the key light. It is used to separate foreground objects from the background. 2) A mortar explosion that is intended to move an object physically during a take.

Kill To stop, turn off or otherwise get rid of a light, sound or vehicle. "Kill the pickup truck now!"

Kinetoscope One of the first cameras used for capturing motion pictures, built by Thomas Edison in the 1890's.

Knuckle Round metal clamp used in conjunction with C-stands, baby plates, gobo arms, etc.

Lamp Op A lamp operator is part of the electrics crew, and is often assigned to setting up and monitoring one or more lights on a set.

Lavalier (lav) See *wire*.

Leader A segment, usually at the beginning of a videotape or film that is just a black screen with no sound.

Letterbox A method of showing a feature film widescreen image on television, by making the picture smaller and putting black areas on the top and bottom of the screen.

Library Shot See *stock footage*.

Limbo This term refers to the absence of reference. A scene is shot in limbo when there is no reference to the surrounding environment, like one shot against total black.

Limpet Mount Named after the gastropod creature of the same name, this is a camera mount that can stick onto any flat surface, such as a car hood.

Linear Editing The old-fashioned way of editing, in one continuous line from beginning to end. See also *non-linear editing*.

Line Producer Producer in charge of the actual finances and day to day supervision of spending and costs on a film production.

Liner A back light, similar to a kicker but on the same side as a key light.

Lip Synch When an actor synchronises his mouth and lip movements to an audio playback.

Location Place of filming that is not on a studio lot or sound-stage.

Location Fee A fee paid to the owner of a location that is used in the production of a film.

Location Manager (L.M.) Person in charge of finding locations to the satisfaction of the director (whether by existing files or scouting), striking deals with property owners, and ensuring a minimum of damage occurs to locations while shooting takes place. They also deal with permits, insurance and abnormal locations requests from various department heads, like blowing up a bus on a major city bridge or shooting late at night in residential neighbourhoods.

Location Scout Person who finds and photographs possible locations under the supervision of the location manager.

Lock it up Prevent any activity or disruption that could interfere with the shot. Generally applies to pedestrians, vehicle traffic and noise in general.

Looping The act of re-recording an actor's lines in a studio while he matches his or her voice to the screen, often at great expense to the production and sometimes months from when the scene was originally shot.

Losing the light A common problem for filmmakers shooting outside or on location when the natural light from the sun is quickly going away.

L.S. Long Shot.

Behind the Scenes

A **Sound Mixer** monitors the sound as the crew films a scene on location.
Photo by Tim Moshansky

A **Steadicam Operator** and **Grip** rehearse a tricky move off of a sweeping crane before rolling the camera.
Photo by Tim Moshansky

Photo 1

Photo 2

Photo 3

The Stunt

Photo 1: *Standby*. The **First Assistant Director** consults with the crew just prior to the stunt. The camera crew waits to the right of the picture.

Photo 2: *Rolling*. The **Stuntman** prepares to jump off of a pipe bridge into the river 95 feet below. With only one take, there's no room for error.

Photo 3: *Action!* The **Stuntman** is just a blur as he jumps off of the bridge and completes his stunt.

Photos by Tim Moshansky

The ever important **Dash Card**, used to identify crew vehicles while shooting on location.
Photo by Shane Harvey

A long **Dolly Track** is laid out as a crew gets ready to shoot a scene in the heart of the urban jungle.
Photo by Shane Harvey

A crew **Blocks the Shot** on an interior stage set
while filming for a t.v. series.
Photo by Shane Harvey.

m

M & E Music and effects. When doing the final sound mix for a film, all of the sounds are broken down into three categories: dialogue, music and effects.

MacGuffin The catalyst for action or a sequence of events in a Hitchcock movie. A MacGuffin is usually a thing that has nothing to do with the characters or building of suspense, but it is what drives the plot along. (For example, the uranium ore in *Notorious* or the secret airplane plans in *The 39 Steps.*)

Mae West Shot A shot that frames an actor from the top of their head to just below their chest.

Magazine The canister that holds the film in a motion picture camera. Also called a *mag.*

Magic Arm Leg Three legged stand used by grips for small, confined spaces.

Magic Hour That part of the day just before sunset when everything is bathed in a golden light.

Mag Stock Film stock used for sound tracks, usually dubbed from a Nagra or DAT machine, so it may be synchronised to the visual portion of a film. Also referred to as mag.

Maquette Small doll or puppet used by special effects people.

Mark 1) When a camera assistant holds the slate in front of the lens before a take, he calls out "mark" just before he claps the sticks together. 2) A tape or chalk mark used so an actor can hit a specific spot during a take.

Martini Shot See *window shot.*

Married When a film's audio and visual portions are put together, the result is called a *married print*.

Mask A blocking device attached to the front of the camera. This technique is often used to give the impression that someone is looking through a telescope or binoculars.

Master Shot A wide or main shot of a scene which is inserted or supplemented with other camera shots in the editing room.

Match When a key position on a film is taken by someone from out of the country, unions require a "match" for that person in the same category. For instance, if a sound effects recordist is brought to Canada from L.A., a *match mixer* is hired to assist them and be their "shadow" for the duration of the time they are there.

Match Dissolve A dissolve in which two images that are similar in size and balance dissolve into each other.

Matte A mask used on the camera or optical printer to prevent certain areas from being exposed, which are used later to insert other backgrounds.

Matte Box A box-like device that fits at the end of a camera lens to protect it from light reflections and provides a receptacle for filters and special effects mattes.

Matte Painting A painting that can be used to simulate a real background, so that moving images may be overlaid on top of it.

M.C.U. Medium close-up.

Meat Axe An adjustable device that clamps onto catwalks to mount lights, etc.

Method Acting An acting or performance style that requires total commitment on the part of the actor to literally become whatever physical or mental state their character is in. If their character is tired, they stay up for 24 hours, if they're hungry, they don't eat for three days. This approach to acting was created and refined in New York, through acting mentor Stanislavsky.

Mickey Mousing Background music that takes its cue directly from the action on the screen, mimicking its every move. This term comes from the early cartoons such as Mickey Mouse, and the technique was later used heavily in Bugs Bunny and other shows.

Mickey Rooney A very slow and short dolly move, i.e. "a little creep."

Miller's Triangle A theoretical triangle which represents green, blue and red, and is applied to black and white photography. The idea is that as you add a filter of one of the colours it diminishes that hue and brings up the others.

Miniature A small model replica of a building or vehicle that is doubling as the real thing in a movie.

Mini Move TO SET A move of only the core production vehicles, not the entire unit, while filming on location.

Mirror Shot A shot that looks into a mirror.

Mise-en-scene The complete, visual presentation of a scene, with the combined elements of lighting, costumes, sets, actors, etc.

Mo See *day mo*.

Mo Ho Slang term for a motorhome, which is often used on tv commercial shoots as the production office, makeup/ wardrobe trailer and film crew headquarters.

M.O.L. "Mit Out Light," is a derivation of M.O.S., and refers to a scene requiring no artificial light.

Montage From the French word *monter* (literally, "to mount"), this is a sequence of shots, or a way of utilising editing to create a certain effect. Russian film great Sergei Eisenstein was one of the first filmmakers to really explore the possibilities of montage in the early part of this century.

Mook A totally green or low on the totem pole crew member.

Morph To have one object visually transform into another object through the use of a computer.

M.O.S. A camera shot that requires no sound to be recorded. From the early German directors' use of the phrase, "mit out sound."

Moviola A film projection device used to view film during the editing process.

M.O.W. Movie of the Week.

M.P. Meal Penalty. One good thing about most film unions is that they make sure crew members have to get a meal after working a certain number of hours or be paid a penalty if they go past it.

Murmur Crowd background noise that is quiet and indiscernible. See also walla and babble.

n

NABET National Association of Broadcast Employees and Technicians.

Nagra Swiss made analogue tape recorder, used almost exclusively for the past 30 years to record dialogue, sound and sound effects on a film production. (pronounced nag-ra or naw-gra)

Narration Spoken-word recording or commentary that is layered onto a visual image. Narration is often used in documentaries, nature films and news programs. See also *voice-over*.

ND Filter Colourless filter that reduces the amount of light entering a camera lens.

N.D. Nondescript. Usually applies to a generic car or extra needed for a scene. (i.e. "Bring me five ND people and one ND car for this shot")

N.F.B. The National Film Board of Canada.

N.G. No good.

N.F.G. No #$%@*! good.

Non-Linear Editing A modern method of editing that utilises computer workstations to edit a film or video. Footage may be stored in the computer and assembled in any order. If the resulting edits are not quite right , they can be stored in the memory on the computer and shuffled around very easily.

O

Oater Another word for a western movie.

Obie Light A small light mounted on the camera to light up an actor's eyes. It was originally designed by cinematographer Lucien Ballard for his actress-wife, Merle Oberon. See also *eyelight*.

Off Line Editing Basically a rough edit that uses safe "work copies" of the audio and visual material of a film before a final cut is made with the master film stock. A computer is generally used to keep track of where the cuts occur, called an Edit Decision List, or EDL.

One-er A shot that may be finished off with only one camera set-up.

One Liner 1) A short joke from a comedian. 2) A preproduction schedule that breaks each scene down into one line that describes it, such as "John tells Jackie that he doesn't have the rent money." It also includes scene numbers, set, actors needed, etc.

On Line Editing When editing is done using the original footage for a final master edit of the movie or video. When completed, the final product will be of "broadcast quality," ready to be copied and distributed to waiting audiences.

On Spec To offer your services on a project without being paid until the project gets off the ground or makes money at some point down the road. This kind of work is speculative because there is no guarantee that you will be ever paid.

On the Clock When a crew is officially being paid for their services, like at the beginning of a day or after lunch.

On the Day When we actually roll the cameras, as in, "O.K., *on the day* we'll drive the car through this wall and out onto the street."

On the Move A phrase used on a set when the crew is changing set-ups or moving to a different location.

Op Short for *operator*, as in camera op, or light op.

Optical An effect that uses an optical print to add other layers onto the film.

Optical Printer A special printer that can combine two or more images for special effects, titles, superimpositions, split screen or a myriad of other invaluable photographic effects not possible with a normal film image.

O.S. Off-screen. In a script, a line of dialogue or action that is not seen by the camera, but affects the action that is on-screen.

Outline A rough sketch of a script.

Out-take A shot that is not used in the final show.

Overlap Sound or image that is laid on top of another for editing purposes.

Over Scale When a performer or crew member becomes quite established in the industry, they often negotiate a higher rate of pay than what is the "scale" rate for that position. See also *scale*.

Over the Shoulder A shot often used when two people are having a conversation in a film. It incorporates part of the listener's shoulder while framing the speaker, to give the impression of being there.

p

P.A. 1) Production assistant. Person employed to help out a film production in so many ways it would be impossible to list them all here. Duties could include crowd control, security, clean-up, public relations, traffic control, keeping crew members quiet, and many other tasks. 2) Public address. An audio system consisting of a microphone, amplifier and speakers.

Pan 1) A camera movement from left to right, or vice versa. 2) When a critic gives a bad review of a movie.

Pancake A small, thin rectangular box used for elevating pieces of gear.

Pass-bys People or vehicles that pass through the frame to create a feeling of realism.

PAR Parabolic Aluminised Reflector. A light that has a self-contained reflector and lens.

Parallel Editing A technique developed by D.W. Griffiths that uses direct cutting between two simultaneously occurring scenes to heighten suspense or climactic excitement.

Pattern Budget On a t.v. series, each head of department provides a budget before the series starts that is an estimate of what they think each episode will cost for them.

Peewee 1) Small camera dolly. 2) A small light.

Pepper Small (100w) light used to illuminate tiny crooks and crannies.

Per Diem Money paid daily to crew members for meals and expenses while shooting out of town.

Pick-Up Shot A shot that must be added to the schedule because there is something missing that needs to be "picked up" before the show wraps.

Picture Car Car or vehicle that is used in a film.

Photo Double A person who dresses and has their makeup and hair done to look exactly like a lead cast member. A photo double is often used for 2nd Unit shots where the camera is on such a long lens that you really can't see for sure who it is anyway.

Picture's Up When rehearsals are over, and the crew is getting ready to roll right away.

Pitch To present a script concept or actor/writer/director package in verbal form to a producer or financier. It basically boils down to somebody trying to convince someone else to put money into a project.

Pilot The first program in a television series, generally a two-hour, made-for-t.v. movie.

Playback Sound or visuals that are "played back" during a take, such as music for rock videos or a t.v. segment that is part of the shot.

Pop A close up shot which does not necessarily cover the entire scene. "We can probably cover this scene with a master shot and a couple of pops."

Pork chop A small board that attaches to dollies for the camera operator to stand on. Named because of its strange shape resembling a pork product.

Poor Man's Process (PMP) A way of creating the illusion of movement for an interior scene in a car by shaking it up and down and flashing lights and shadows across it.

Post Production The part of a production that includes the editing and finishing aspects of a production, after all of the scenes have been shot. May be subdivided into audio and visual editing, packaging, distribution, etc.

POV Point of View. Shot that assumes the character's line of vision in a scene. "Let's turn it around now and get his POV of the room."

Practical Anything that is operational on a set, like a table lamp or a kitchen sink.

Pre-Production Everything that must be taken care of before shooting starts, including casting, hiring of department heads, shooting schedule, script breakdown, scouting and securing locations, securing financing and many other details. Usually, the more time spent and effort spent in pre-production, the more smoothly the production will go.

Pretties Slang for the Hair, Make-up and Wardrobe departments. Sometimes used to refer to the trucks that are used by these departments.

Primacord Highly explosive cord of various grains used by the special effects crew to blow things up.

Primes The lenses most used and needed by a camera crew.

Principal A main actor or character in a show. Not to be confused with a bit part actor or, heaven forbid, an extra.

Process Shot A technique of filming that combines live action with a projected background. This technique was used a lot in the old days when shooting actors in a car, with a moving background projected on a screen behind the car.

Producer $ Person who oversees all aspects of a production at every stage along the way. The producer locks in the financing for each project, as well as being involved in creative decisions such as script rewrites, who will be cast in the movie, and how the film will be distributed.

Production Co-ordinator (P.C.) Person who runs the production office under the guidelines of the production manager. Tasks may include organising equipment rentals, customs brokers, hotel rooms for actors and directors, relaying messages to and from set, and a myriad of other duties, many of which are assigned to the assistant production co-ordinator or the office P.A.

Production Designer Person who, in conjunction with the art director, is responsible for the entire visual look of a film, and makes decisions about set decoration, props, make-up and wardrobe in the pre-production phase and supervises these elements during shooting.

Production Manager (P.M.) $ Person who ensures the production runs smoothly and as planned, always keeping a close eye on budget and unnecessary expenses, such as time delays.

Production Report A daily report of what scenes were shot, how much film was shot, in and out times for all crew members and actors, and comments on special circumstances or problems that may have delayed the production.

Production Schedule A detailed breakdown of a film's shooting schedule that outlines each day of production including info about which scenes will be shot on which days, and which actors, props and locations are required for those days.

Product Placement To prominently feature or display a product such as a can of soda in a film or tv show. Large sums of money have been paid by advertisers to film companies to show famous actors using their products on camera.

Prop Slang for *property*. Any object used in a film designated by the script or the director to be used by an actor in a scene. This may include anything the imagination may come up with, including fake food, weapons, condoms, staplers or cash registers.

Prop Buyer Person employed, under the supervision of the propmaster, to acquire props to be used in a film.

Property Master Usually called a propmaster, this is the person in charge of acquiring props as required by the script and overseeing their use during a production. Propmasters and their assistants are almost always firearms technicians, trained in the safe use of guns and ammunition.

Pull Focus See *rack*.

Pump Cup A small suction cup that is "pumped" to hold the cup to a wall, ceiling or other flat surface to attach lights, flags, etc.

Push 1) When a shooting schedule is moved ahead for whatever reason. 2) Overdeveloping film in the lab to compensate for low lighting conditions.

P.Z.M. Pressure zone microphone. A flat microphone that is usually taped to a piece of plexiglass to record extremely loud sounds such as gunblasts and explosions.

q

Quartz Lamp A specific type of lamp that uses a quartz filament for a constant colour temperature.

Quick Study When an actor reads a specific portion of a script in a hurried fashion to get the gist of a scene.

A **Camera Assistant** gets a little wet as a crew gets ready to film an underwater shot. *Photo by Shane Harvey.*

Rack When a camera changes, or "pulls" focus from one object to another during a shot. Also known as a *pull focus*, or *rack focus*.

Rain Towers Huge metal tube towers set up by the FX dept. to simulate rain on a set, from a slight drizzle to a torrential downpour.

Rake A camera or lighting angle that is neither head-on nor a profile, but rather a diagonal.

Raw Footage Unedited film footage.

Raw Stock Unexposed film stock.

Rear Screen Projection A method of projecting an image onto an opaque screen meant to be played behind the subject that is being filmed. This technique was used extensively in the 50's and 60's whenever an actor was driving a car. The scene was usually filmed on a sound stage with a rear screen projection of a moving background playing behind the car, giving the illusion of movement. Although it looked a little cheesy back then, rear screen technology has vastly improved since then and is still in use today. See also *process shot*.

Redhead A small light named for its red casing.

Release Print The print of a film or video that is released for distribution to t.v. stations or movie theatres.

Reverse Angle To flip the camera around 180 degrees to shoot the reverse of what it was previously filming.

Reset After a take has been done, the 1st A.D. will often call for a reset to bring actors, vehicles and extras back to their original positions for another take. Also called *first positions, back to one, going again* or *number ones.*

Residuals Money paid to a performer or crew member every time the production is broadcast, in addition to the original amount they were paid. TV commercials and series can be quite lucrative to anyone who has residuals built into their contract for a production.

Ripple Dissolve Popularised in recent times by Wayne and Garth of Wayne's World, the ripple dissolve is a blending of two images with a ripple effect, often denoting a transition into a dream or flashback.

Rocker See *gimbal.*

Rolling When you hear this word on a set, it means that the camera, and usually sound, are running. "We're rolling ... Speed!...Scene four take twelve 'A' only, mark...And, action!"

Rough Cut A temporary edit of a film or video with some rough edges that are to be worked out.

Rumble Pot A device used for creating a low lying fog on movie sets. The container boils water, and then a basket full of crushed dry ice is lowered into the water, creating a low ground fog cloud. The pot makes a lot of rumbling, bubbling sounds, hence its name.

Rushes See *dailies.*

S.A.G. Screen Actors Guild. (U.S.)

Sandbag A small sack of canvas or leather filled with sand which anchors stands and sets from falling over, and is also used as a mark for actors or vehicles.

Scale A set rate of pay for a writer, performer or crew member, as determined by their union or guild.

Scene A segment of a film or t.v. show that is composed of a series of shots, and usually takes place in one time and place

Schenkeling To "schenkel" means that the crew will be asked to set up for shooting on the next set before finishing shooting on the present set, i.e. working two sets at a time. It is named after the director Carl Schenkel who does this on a regular basis.

Scooch To move an object or actor. Similar to "cheat."

Scoop A studio lamp with a soft, wide throw of 500 to 2000 watts.

Score 1) Musical composition that is layered into the soundtrack of a film. 2) Actual written piece of music that is used by musicians to play the music.

Scout TO SET To physically go and look at potential locations for a project. See also *location scout.*

Script Supervisor The person responsible for keeping track of the take and roll numbers, camera and sound reloads, script revisions, how long each take lasts, scene numbers, slate numbers, prompting the actor(s) when they forget their lines, and making sure that continuity is upheld between takes and different angles. Also called a *continuity person*.

Second Assistant Director (2nd A.D.) The person responsible for preparing the call sheet in consultation with the 1st A.D., arranging for pick-ups and drop-offs of actors and for calling in to the production office to alert them on the progress of the shooting day (first shot times, meal penalties, etc.).

Second Meal When a crew works a certain amount of hours past lunch, a second meal is prepared or ordered for the crew.

Second Team See *stand-in*.

Second Unit A separate, smaller crew on a production that is responsible for getting establishing shots, or any shots that were not achieved with the main unit.

S.E.G. Screen Extras Guild. (U.S.)

Segue A musical or visual cue that carries from one transition to the next without interruption.(pronounced *seg-way*)

Sensitive Location TO SET A location such as a park or an expensive home where extra care must be taken not to damage or destroy walls, trees, furniture, etc.

Set TO SET The place, either on location or in a studio, where a t.v. show or movie is filmed.

Set Dec Short for Set Decoration, this is the department responsible for how a set looks during a shot.

Set Dresser Person who "dresses the set" with decorations, artwork, rugs, etc. Sometimes called an on-set dresser, this person must supervise the continuity of sets under the supervision of the set decorator or art director.

Scrim Round stainless steel screens that go in front of lights to reduce the intensity of the brightness.

Shooting ratio A mathematical ratio of how much film was shot versus how much is used in the final program. The smaller the ratio (i.e. 4:1 or 3:1) the more economical the shoot.

Shop To actively push a new project or series in order to get it sold or produced. This is similar in many ways to a musician or band *shopping* their music demo to various record labels to get a deal.

Shop Steward Person that represents the crew from a union perspective, ensuring that people receive proper turn-around, overtime and working conditions. This person is usually a crew member on the show.

Shotgun Mic A long, cylindrical directional microphone that is used for recording distant sounds.

Sides A small photocopied version of the day's call sheet and relevant pages of the script used by actors, directors and other crew members to refer to while on set.

Sight Line The direction an actor is looking during a shot. It can be very important to keep an actor's sightline clear to ensure he or she can concentrate properly. Also called an *eyeline*.

Slate Small blackboard with spaces for the title of the production, the scene number, the take number, the cameraman's name and the name of the production company producing the film. When both the camera and tape recorder are running at speed, the director instructs the assistant to "mark it," or "slate it," with a clap of the two pieces of board, before calling "action." Used to synchronise the sound with the picture when editing later on. See also *clapper*.

Slate-in When auditioning before a camera, an actor is expected to give his or her name, age, agent's name and other important details so they may be referred to later.

Sleeper A movie released by the studios that is not expected to do really well.

Slug A piece of film which will be replaced at a later date that is inserted in a work print.

Slush Truck Truck used to haul miscellaneous items such as chairs, tables, heaters, fans and tarps. Also called a *gak truck*.

SMPTE Society of Motion Picture and Television Engineers. This is also the name given to a type of time code striped onto video tape for syncing purposes.

Snoot Funnel shaped device attached to lamps instead of barn doors for a more precise light beam.

Snot Sticky putty used by set dec and grips to temporarily hold various items in place.

S.O.C. Silent On Camera. When an actor is used in a scene more prominently than a typical extra but doesn't have any spoken lines, a "silent on camera" credit and wage upgrade is given to that person. This term is used mostly for commercials.

Soft Focus A method of filming that purposely leaves part or all of the frame out of focus to achieve a "soft" effect on the subject. This can be achieved in a number of different ways, including filters, Vaseline on a piece of glass over the lens, or a focusing of the lens itself.

Soubrette An actress playing a young, flirtatious woman.

Sound Mixer The person in charge of recording all of the sound on a movie set, including dialog, sound effects and room tone, as well as alerting the director as to what will and will not be a usable sound take during a shot.

Sound Optical The use of sound to create a layered effect in the editing process, much like an optical effect would do for a visual image. For example, a soundtrack that continues from one scene to the next, even though the visual image has changed is called a *sound optical.*

Sound Stage A studio where scenes involving dialogue are filmed.

Source Music Music in a film or video that comes from something seen or implied onscreen, such as a radio, tape or CD player, jukebox or musician. Does not apply to background or theme music that is simply added to the soundtrack. Also called *actual music.*

SPFX See *special effects.*

Spaghetti with pizza on the side Slang term for a dolly track with a dolly set on top of it (the operator's chair is round).

Sparrow Plate A small, narrow plate used by grips to mount flags, lights or other devices.

Special Effects The department that deals with explosions, squibs, blood packets, rain, snow, wind, fog and many other pyrotechnic and visual effects. Also known as *SPFX* or *FX*.

Special Effects Co-Ordinator The person in charge of the FX department. The co-ordinator must be extremely knowledgeable about explosives, rigging and safety as he or she often has to deal with dangerous circumstances and unpredictability.

Speed Word yelled out by the sound mixer when his tape recorder is rolling. This term dates back to the old studio days when the crew literally had to get an electrical charge built up to a certain rate before they could power the cameras.

Spider Three strips of plastic or metal that spread out the legs of a tripod. Also called a *spreader*.

Spin Off A television show or movie that comes from another show. For instance, the popular t.v. series *Frasier* is a *spin off* of the immensely successful *Cheers!*

Splinter Unit Part of the main unit of a production that breaks away to do other setups and shots at a different location. Also called a *swing unit*.

Split Screen A technique used to divide a scene into multiple images, so an actor may play a dual role on the same screen, or to give the impression that an actor is in the same shot as a dangerous animal.

Spot A tv or radio commercial. A spot can be also referred to as :15, :30, or :60 to denote a fifteen, thirty or sixty second commercial.

Spot Meter A device used by cinematographers that measures reflective light within a narrow field of view.

Spotting When doing the editing or sound editing on a film, a spotting session is done to make notes on what will be required in the post production process (such as possible problems with dialog or missing shots).

Squib A small explosive charge that is planted and camouflaged on an area where a gunshot is supposed to hit. A squib is generally wired or connected to a remote control device and then discharged at the appropriate time by a special effects person.

S.S.E. Special Skills Extra. If an extra is required to do something in a scene that requires a skill such as playing an instrument or riding a bike, an upgrade is given to them.

Stand-by Be prepared for shooting—everything is in place and the 1st A.D. has their hand on the trigger finger.

Standby Painter The person who is in charge of all painting and spray bombing on a movie set. Whether it is touch ups of furniture or scenery or even the grass, the standby painter must be ready to colour our world at an instant's notice.

Stand-in A person who stands in the place of the principal actors while the cameras and lights are set up. This gives the actors a chance to take a break, practise their lines or graze at craft service. Also referred to as *second team*.

Starlight A truck that has its own generator, light and crane to provide night lighting for exterior shots.

Start Pack Bundle of papers that must be filled out by cast and crew members when beginning work on a film production. The start pack includes a tax form, deal memo, safety guidelines, start slip and many other bureaucratic forms.

Starwagon Large trailer that houses temporary rooms for actors while filming on location.

Steadicam Camera stabilising device developed in the seventies that hooks up to the operator's body with a harness. It allows for moving the camera without using dollies or cranes, giving a smooth flowing image throughout a scene (i.e. running up stairs, going in and out of elevators.) Often used as a POV camera.

Sticks 1) Slang term for a tripod. 2) Slang term for the clapper, or clapboard.

Stills As opposed to moving pictures, stills are photographs taken for promotional material and publications.

Still Photographer Person responsible for taking pictures of actors and sets during filming.

Stipple The technique used by makeup artists to apply facial hair on actors such as moustaches and beards.

Stock Footage Archived footage that is stored and sold to filmmakers. Stock footage may included shots of cityscapes, H-bomb explosions, volcanoes, or other shots that may be hard to get or costly to reproduce.

Stop-Motion A form of animation which uses small puppets shot one painstaking frame at a time to achieve the look of fluid motion when projected at the standard 24 frames per second.

Storyboard Sequence of drawings in comic book format that is assembled before attempting a shot for real, so the director and his or her crew are sure of what and how they are going to shoot.

Strike To disassemble or take down a set after filming is completed.

Stunt Any type of action during a scene that involves the possibility of an actor being hurt, such as fighting, falling from a building or jumping from a moving car.

Stunt Adjustment An extra amount of cash given to a stunt person depending on the severity of a stunt. Some stunt people have received several thousands of dollars for one stunt because they risked their lives doing it.

Stunt Co-ordinator The person who prepares and organises all stunts on a movie, whether they be horse falls, fights, car chases, building falls, or any action sequence which involves the possibility of an actor or stunt double getting hurt. Every move is planned and rehearsed in consultation with the director and the 1st A.D. to get the right look for the shot, but also to provide complete safety to all of the cast and crew.

Stunt Double A person who is made up and dressed to look like an actor for a stunt or action scene.

Sugar Glass A sugar based glass that was used in the past as a safe substitute for real glass.

Superimpose To blend an image right over top of another one. This may apply to titles, credits or live action photography. Godzilla was often superimposed onto a Japanese city background, as he waded through the buildings to the centre of town.

Survey See *scout*.

Sweetening The process whereby the audio track for a film is cleaned up and prepared for a final release.

Swish Pan An effect in which the camera is swung very rapidly in a panning motion, producing a blurred image. Also called a *zoom pan, zip pan, flick pan, flash pan* or *whip pan*.

Switcher Person or device that takes two or more incoming video signals (usually from different cameras at, say, a hockey game) and switches between them for a broadcast of one signal.

Sync Synchronise.

Sync Sound Sound that is recorded simultaneously with a moving photographic image. A clapper is used to help synchronise the two in the editing process.

Syndication When a recurring show is shown as re-runs on television, it is known as *syndication*.

Synopsis A brief rundown of a script or story that may be summarised in two or three sentences.

T-Bone A rigid T-shape base, usually nailed to a studio floor for low positioning of lights.

T-Stop The true f/stop number when a lens is free from reflection and absorption loss. (T means transmission and stop means to decrease the amount of light admitted to the film). A T-stop represents the f/number of a lens with 100 percent transmission of the light rays.

Tail Slate Using the clapboard or slate to "mark" the shot after a take. Usually the clapper is held upside down so an editor knows for sure it is a tail slate.

Take One segment of shooting during production. If the take is good, the director will often say "print," which means send the film to be processed and transferred to video to be watched the next day. These are called dailies or rushes. A bad, or "blown" take is often designated as NG, or "no good."

Talent A term used to designate the actors, musicians or stunt people in a film production.

Teamster A member of the Teamster's Union. Teamsters, or "the Brothers" are responsible for driving the production vehicles on a film, including the honeywagons, starwagon, cable truck, cast vehicles, picture cars and pretty much anything else that moves.

Teaser 1) The first part of a tv movie or series episode that is intended to make the viewer want to watch the show. 2) A long, thin piece of wood with a sheet of black Duvetyne cloth attached to it for shading light sources.

Tech Pack The package of drawings of all the floor plans for the sets and final locations on a show.

Tech Survey Once all of the locations have been selected and locked in for a production, a survey of all of the locations is attended by all of the department heads to assess each individual location's requirements and restrictions.

Teleprompter A monitor or computer screen that "prompts" a television host with their lines by printing them out on a screen that they can see but the audience can't.

Temporal Compression A technique used by filmmakers that purposely leaves out chunks of "time" in the telling of a story. A great example of this is in 2001: A Space Odyssey, where Kubrick compresses thousands of years with the shot of an ape throwing a bone into the air cut with a shot of a spaceship.

Third Assistant Director (3rd A.D.) The person responsible for signing in and out the actors and performers on a set, making sure they get into hair, make-up and wardrobe in time for their scenes, escorting them to set, preparing the production report and assisting the 1st and 2nd A.D.'s when needed.

Tight A shot that frames a subject very closely. (e.g., "Let's get a tight shot of her hand.")

Tilt A vertical camera movement, either up or down.

Time Code A code of numbers that is used to synchronise sound and picture for a film, and to keep track of the time and place of various segments during the editing process.

Time Lapse Shooting at a much slower rate than the normal time speed of 24 frames per second. This technique is often used in nature programs to show a flower growing out of the ground.

Touch Paper Paper that has been treated with potassium nitrate by the special effects crew. When touched with a cigarette or hot wire, the paper will ignite and burn along the line of solution applied to the paper. This effect has sometimes been used for main titles.

Tow Shot When filming one or more actors while driving a car, the car is often towed on a trailer to enable the actors to concentrate on acting rather than driving,and to light and shoot the scene more easily.

Tracking Shot A moving camera shot, usually achieved with a camera mounted on a dolly which is in turn mounted on a track.

Trailer An advertisement for a film that is shown before the screening of another film. A trailer is usually a short clip of the most stunning shots of a film edited together with sound, music and narration that says how great the film is.

Trainee Assistant Director (TAD) TO SET The trainee, or TAD, assists the other assistant directors in carrying out sometimes mundane but important tasks like getting the stars their breakfasts, issuing walkie-talkies and batteries to crew members, watching the lunch line-up, cueing extras, writing down wrap times for various crew members, handing out call sheets and other duties.

Trainee Assistant Locations (TAL) Someone who is training to be an Assistant Location Manager.

Translight A large, transparent photograph that is used as a background on soundstages. For instance, translights are used to simulate an exterior such as a skyline without having to shoot near the actual skyline.

Transport Captain The person that supervises all vehicle requirements while on set.

Transport Co-ordinator The person responsible for organising and scheduling all vehicles and drivers for a motion picture.

Treatment A script form that is somewhere between a rough outline and a completed script.

Trombone A bracket that hangs on a wall to hold a small lamp.

Tulip Crane A small see-saw type camera crane with weights on one end and a camera and operator(s) on the other. Used for smooth sweeping and rising shots.

Tungsten A type of light filament used in lighting scenes, characterised by its orange colour tone.

Turnaround Amount of time, regulated by unions, that a production must give its crew between shooting days without going into costly penalties. (Usually 8-10 hours between days and at least 52 hours for weekends.)

Turn Over See *rolling*. This term originated in Britian.

Turret A revolving disk system mounted on a camera that may be turned to use different lenses.

Turtle Base A small, three-legged base that forms the bottom of a C-stand.

Two-shot Camera shot that has two actors in the frame.

Tweenie A 650 watt fresnel light, the in-between (thus tweenie) of a Baby and an Inky.

Tyler Mount A gyroscopic camera mount used to film from helicopters.

U

Ubangi Politically incorrect term for a mount that extends the camera away from its center on the dolly. Allegedly named for the Ubangi people of Africa who extend their lower lip by artificial means.

U.B.C.P. Union of British Columbia Performers.

Unit Manager (U.M.) Person responsible for the requirements of the crew and production when a film is complex enough to require an extensive second shooting crew or when a P.M. needs an assistant for extra duties.

Umbrella Light A lighting device that employs a white mylar umbrella with a tungsten-halogen light attached to its handle and pointing into the centre of the umbrella. This type of soft light is often used as a window light source because of its "wrap around" quality.

Upstage 1) That portion of a set furthest away from the camera. 2) To try to get all of the attention away from another actor.

Tow Shot *Illustration by Kirk Johns*

V

Variac Trade name of a variable transformer (dimmer control) used by the lighting and special effects departments.

Vertigo Shot A camera shot that zooms forward with the lens while tracking or dollying backward. This shot, which conveys a feeling of dizziness, was created for Alfred Hitchcock's masterpiece Vertigo by second-unit cameraman Irmin Roberts. It is one of the most widely imitated shots in film history.

Video Assist A video monitor that connects to the 35mm film camera allowing the director to watch a take as it is being filmed.

Video Sync The synchronisation of an image from a t.v. or computer screen to conform with the 24 fps used by the cameras. If you don't have video sync, you get annoying scan lines moving up or down the screen on the film or video image.

Viewfinder The part of a camera that you look through to see the image.

Vignette A shot that is blurry or fuzzy around the edges and clear and focused in the middle.

Visual Effects Computer graphics and animation that are added in after filming is completed.

Voice Over (V.O.) An audible narration layered into the soundtrack.

W

Walk and Talk Common shot that involves people walking and talking. This is a great way to kill off a big dialogue scene with some movement, used quite often on t.v. movies.

Walla The name given to a track of ambient sound that is layered onto a film, such as the sound of people in a restaurant or sports event to create a "wall" of sound.

Western Dolly Similar in design to a doorway dolly, the western is larger and capable of carrying a heavier load. It can be used as a camera dolly, equipment mover or as a tow platform behind a camera car.

Wedges Small triangular blocks of wood used by grips to elevate or level dolly tracks, apple boxes or other pieces of film gear.

Wescam A camera stabilising device that is used for extremely smooth aerial shots.

Wetdown The dousing of any part of a set (usually streets at night) to create a glossy, reflective look on film.

W.G.A. Writer's Guild of America.

W.G.C. Writer's Guild of Canada.

Wide Screen An aspect ratio that has a larger width than height, such as 16 by 9. See also *letterbox*.

Wide Shot One that is the opposite of a close up, one that covers a lot of area in the frame.

Wild Line (or Wild Track) Sound or dialogue recorded on a set without any cameras rolling, usually to record ambient environment sounds, or to get a better dialogue line.

Wild Wall, Wild Ceilings Walls and ceilings that can be moved on a set at any given moment.

Windjammer Fuzzy tube shaped item placed over a microphone at the end of a boom to decrease wind noise.

Window Shot The last shot of the day. One of the happiest things you can hear after a 15 hour day. ("O.K. everybody, this is the *window shot*, so let's concentrate.") Some people say the term arose out of "when do we go?" but the actual meaning goes back to London in the early, early days of filmmaking when everyone on the crew was paid in cash daily. After the last shot was completed they went to the window to get their payment. Also called a *martini shot* in the U.S.

Winnies Winnebagos. On smaller shoots and some commercials, winnebagos or motor homes are used instead of more costly trailers. The Winnie can be the honeywagon, A.D. box, conference room, wardrobe trailer, and production office all in one. Also called a *moho*.

Wipe 1) An actor or vehicle that crosses the camera frame horizontally. 2) An edit that "wipes" one shot into the next from right to left or vice-versa.

Wire A small microphone and transmitter that is attached to an actor, whose dialogue is then mixed by the sound mixer along with sound recorded by a boom operator. Also called a *lav*, or *lavalier microphone, radio microphone* or *body mic*.

Work Print A copy of the footage from a movie or t.v. show that can be used to try out editing ideas.

Work Trucks The trucks that are worked out of the most—the grip truck, the camera truck, the lighting truck, the FX truck and the props truck. These vehicles are usually parked as close to the set as possible.

Working Title A title given to a project as it is being worked on that may or may not become the actual title of a film.

Wrap The happiest word on a movie set. Done for the day. Finished. Go home and get your three or four hours of sleep.

Wrap Party The party that is generally held after the completion of a film or t.v. series.

Wrangler Person who "wrangles" extras, animals or livestock during the shooting of a film, or person who rounds them up before a shoot.

A portable generator (**Genny)** like this one is one of the most important pieces of gear on a shoot— it provides all of the power for a film set.
Photo by Shane Harvey

Xenon Lamp A special type of light that uses a xenon filament.

X-Rated A pornographic or ultra violent film, now referred to as NC-17 by the American standards board.

X-sheet Animation filming sheet with written exposure specs.

Yagi Fold up antenna device used by the sound department when wireless microphones are employed.

Y-Cable Cable that splits one signal into two, or vice-versa.

Z

Zeppelin Windscreen A blimp-shaped cover that fits over a microphone boom to prevent wind sounds from interfering with the recording.

Zinger Any directional light source used to highlight a scene predominantly lit with soft light.

Zip A 2000 watt narrow softlight, useful in low ceiling situations.

Zoetrope A machine invented in the 1800's that was one of the first motion picture projection devices. Incidentally, Francis Coppola's film company is called *American Zoetrope*.

Zoom 1) A lens movement in or out of a scene. 2) The lens used to perform this movement.

If you would like to receive additional copies of the
A TO Z GUIDE TO FILM TERMS

Send $11.95 plus $2.00 for postage and handling in Canada.

Send $7.95 plus $2.00 for postage and handling in U.S. funds from the U.S. and elsewhere.

By cheque or money order *only*, to:

FIRST WAVE PUBLISHING
P.O. Box 71031-B4
Vancouver B.C. V6N 4J9

Please allow 2-4 weeks for delivery

If you have any comments, or would like to suggest other terms or phrases and their origins, please write to me at the address above or e-mail me at: tim@canadafilm.com

Your feedback is appreciated.

The A.D. *Illustration by Kirk Johns*

10-4 Affirmative. This usually follows a question such as, "do you copy that?"

10-20 The exact location of a person, place or thing. You will often hear "What's your twenty?" over the radio which simply means, "Where are you?"

10-100 Going to the bathroom. this phrase can also be used by a crew member who doesn't want people to know where he or she is.

Copy That A confirmation that someone has heard and understood a message. Sometimes shortened to "copy."

Go to "2" Change your walkie to channel two. Crews usually reserve channel one for important information for the whole crew. Secondary conversations often go to channel two for things that others don't need to hear.

Notes:

Notes:

Notes:

Notes:

A **Camera Operator** makes some final adjustments on a camera that is perched on a **High Hat** mounted on a **1/4 Apple Box.**
Photo by Shane Harvey